One Hundred and One Visual Haiku

volume one   ami fagin

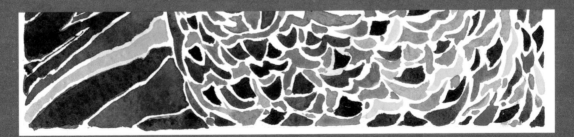

Haley's
Athol, Massachusetts

may you live your life

with artistic precision

sculpting your Divine

my dichotomy

an infinite horizon

step by step forward

to Wayne

sculptor and sailor

problem solver and protector

balancer of
weighty objects and objectives

and

most companionable of companions

#1   BENEATH THE SURFACE

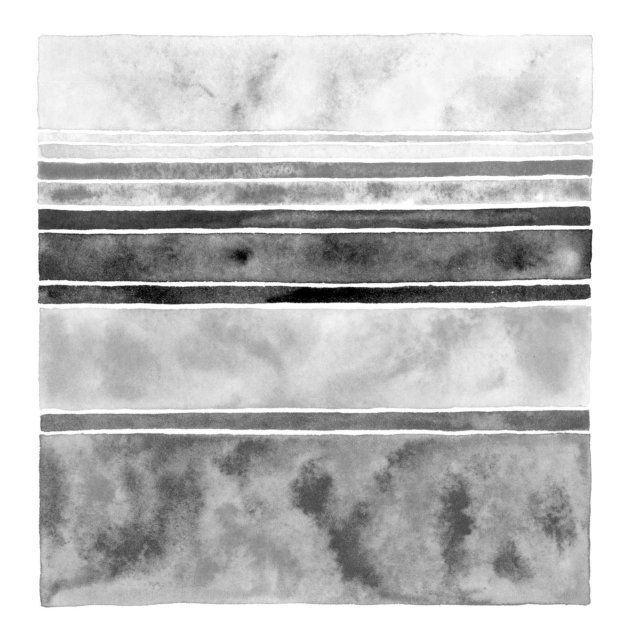

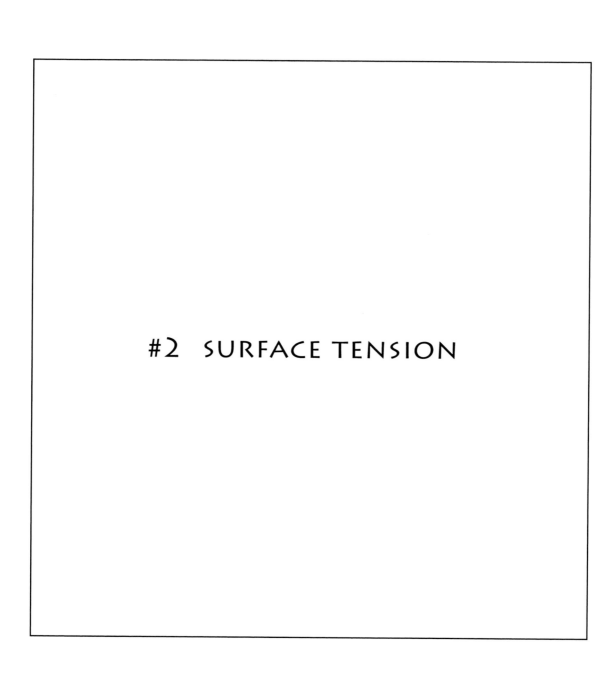

#2 SURFACE TENSION

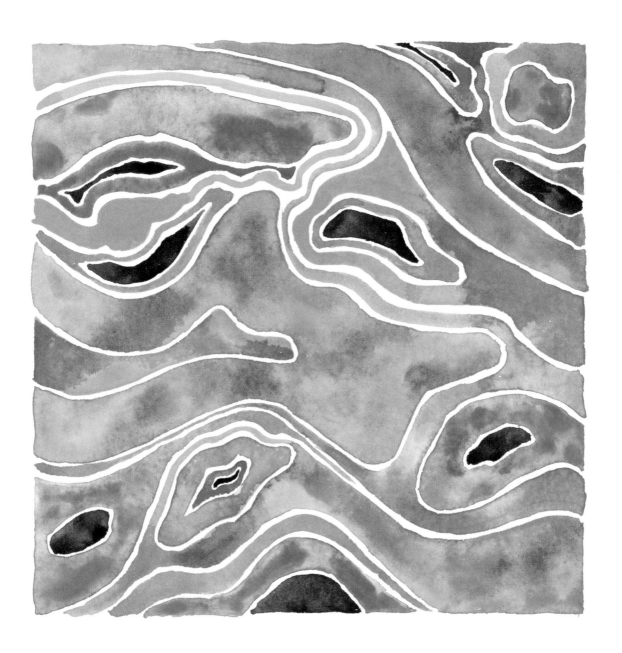

#3 UNDERCURRENTS

#4 APPROACHING FALL

#5 GRASS FIRE

#6 COOLING LAVA

#7 SOCIAL STRATIFICATION

#8 APPROACHING FALL II

#9 DRIVING RAIN

#10 GIRLS JUST WANNA HAVE FUN

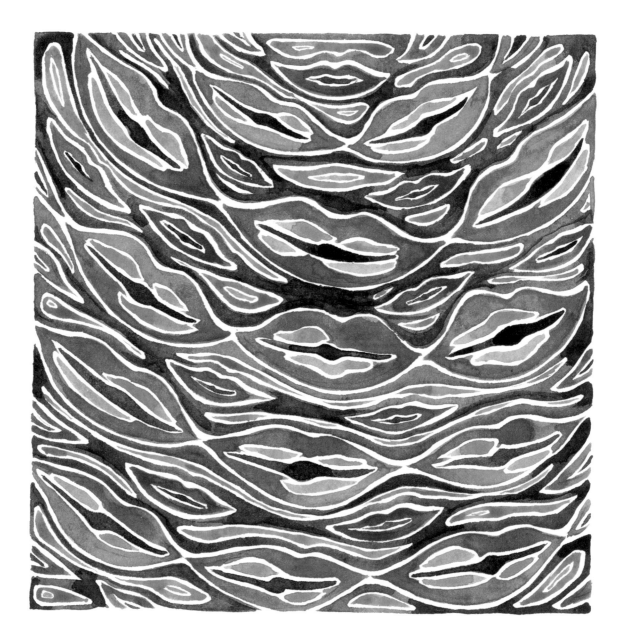

#11 FACING SHADOWS

#12 INSOMNIA

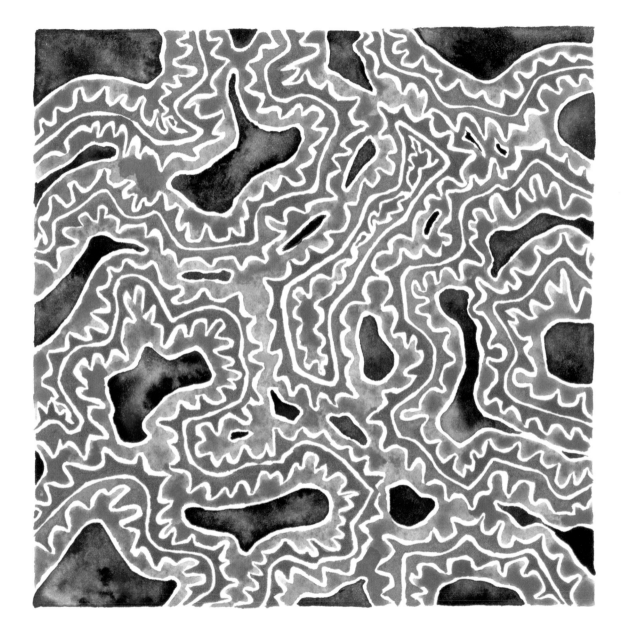

#13 THE BOWL

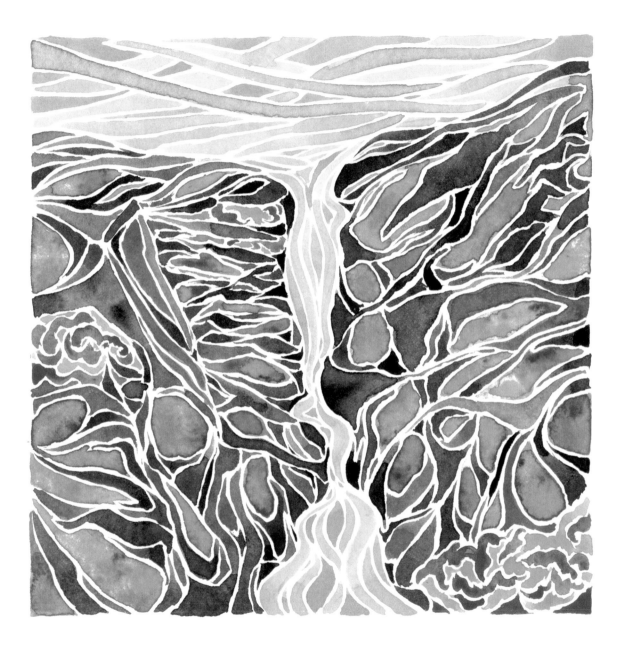

#14 MENTAL ILLNESS

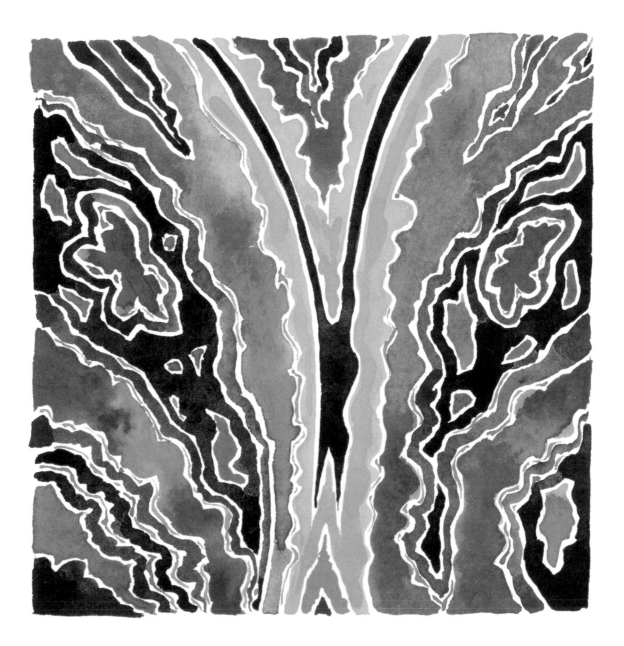

#15 DREAMCATCHER

#16 CHUM

#17 THE DESCENT

#18 MORNING HAS SPOKEN

#19 BOSOM OF MY FAMILY

#20 CROWN OF THORNS

#21 SALT OF THE EARTH

#22 NO WHERE TO RUN

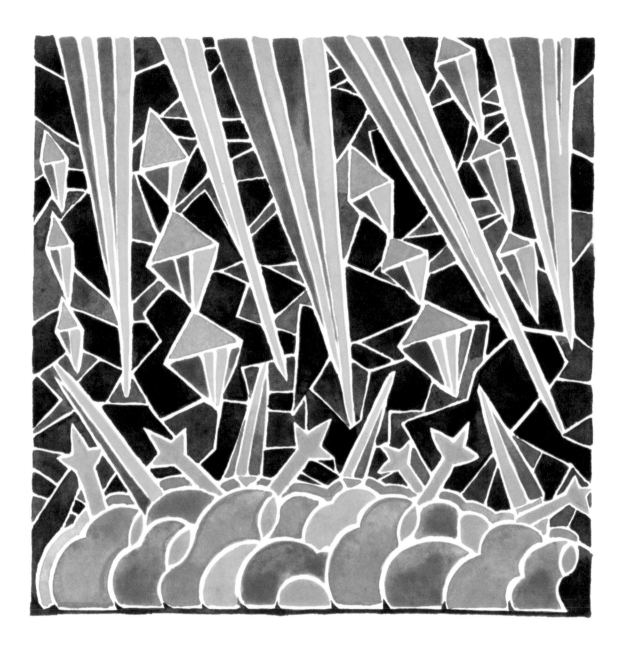

#23 AN ANGRY WOUND

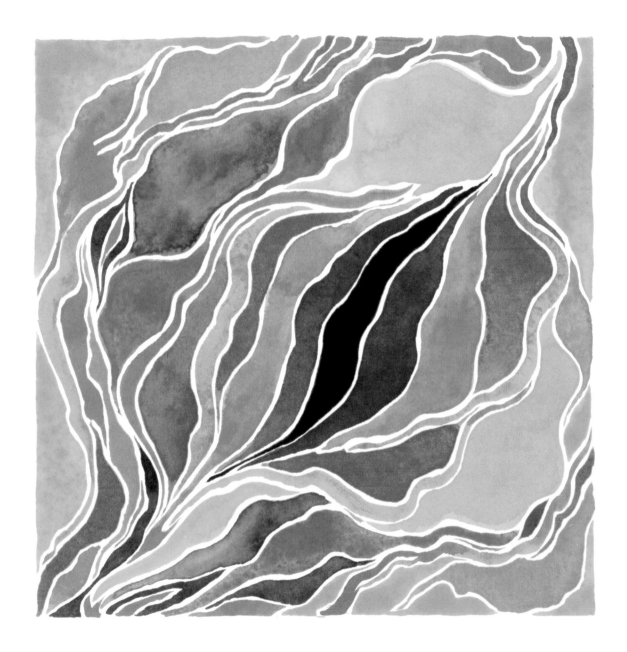

#24 HOSTA

#25 I, REFUGEE: STARVATION

#26 DALE CHIHULY'S GLASS CEILING

#27 APPROACHING FALL III

#28 SHOOTING STARS

#29 BLOOD MOON RISING 9/27/15

#30 APPROACHING FALL IV

#31 COVERED BRIDGE

#32 IN THE PALM OF MY HAND

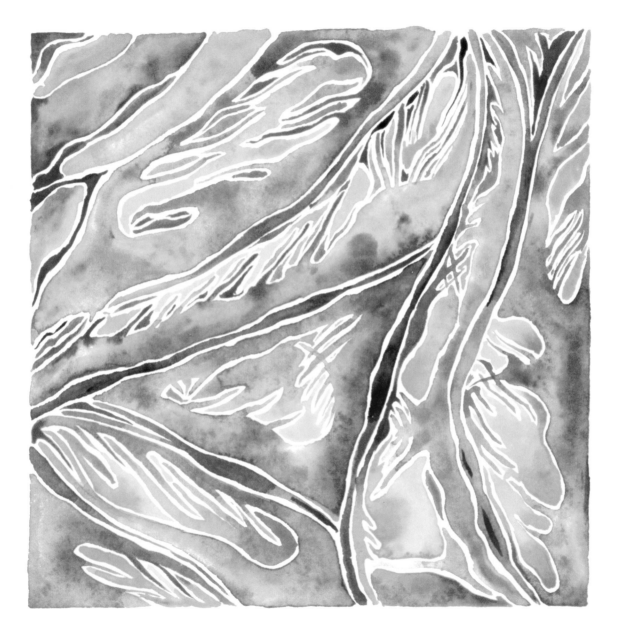

#33 THE MILKY WAY

#34 Sacajawea

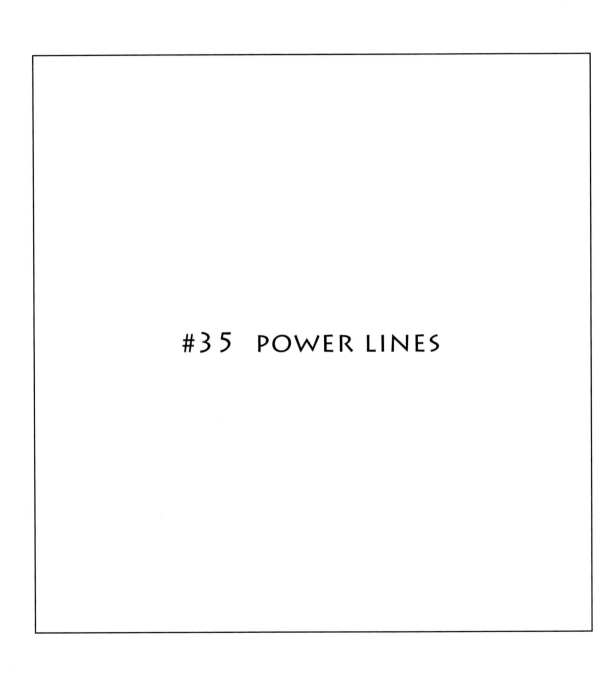

#35 POWER LINES

#36 TWIN BOMBING RUNS AT DAYBREAK

#37 SAMSARA

#38 CORN HARVEST:
A NEW ENGLAND FIELD

#39 WEB OF INTRIGUE

#40 THROUGH THE WOODS

#41 EXPLOSION

#42 Adam's apples

#43 BEER RUN

#44 FERN'S FALL FINALE

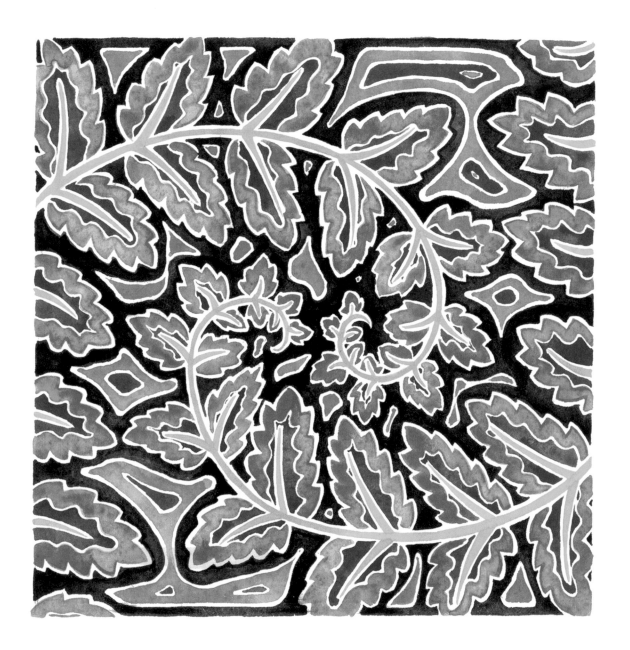

#45 ECONOMIC MIGRATION

#46 ALWAYS A BRIDESMAID

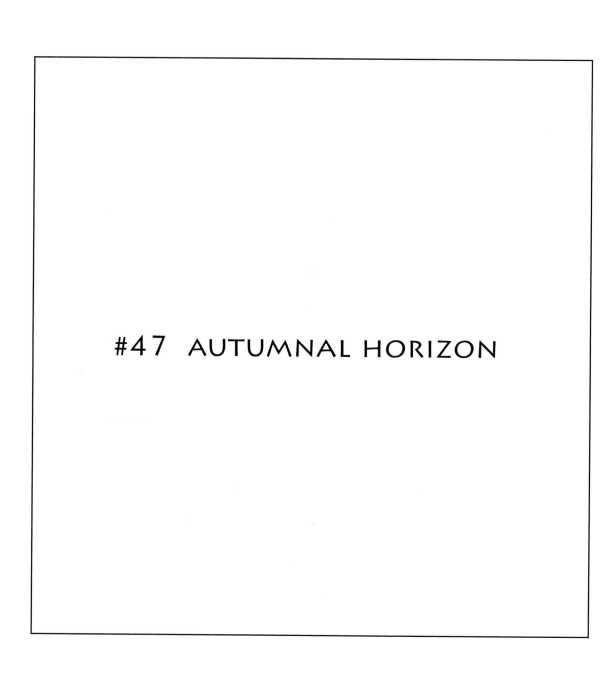

#47 AUTUMNAL HORIZON

#48 FREE RANGE

#49 THE COMMON COLD

#50 Get Lucky Farm

#51 SEASON'S GREETINGS

#52 ROSE WINDOW

#53 THINGS ARE LOOKIN' UP

#54 MORNING LIGHT

#55 LIBRARY POETRY CONTEST
Orange, MA

#56 JOLLY TIME

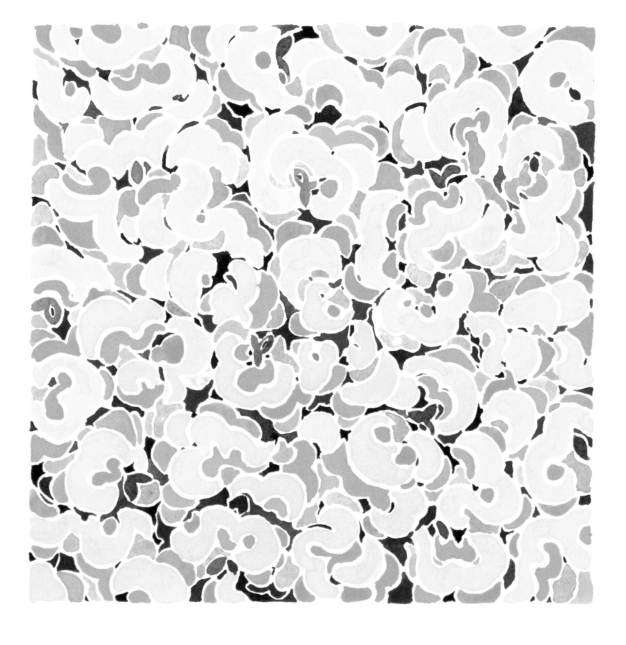

#57 All Hallows' Eve
New Salem center, MA

#58 The Night of Broken Glass

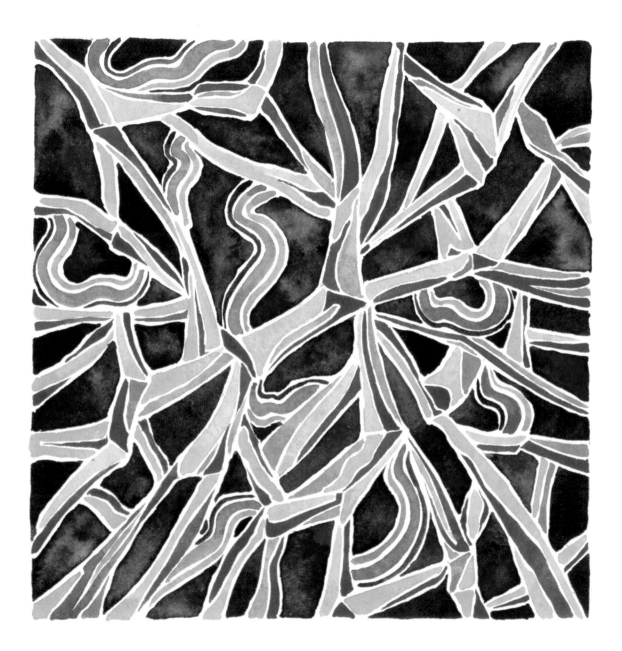

#59 UP AGAINST A WALL

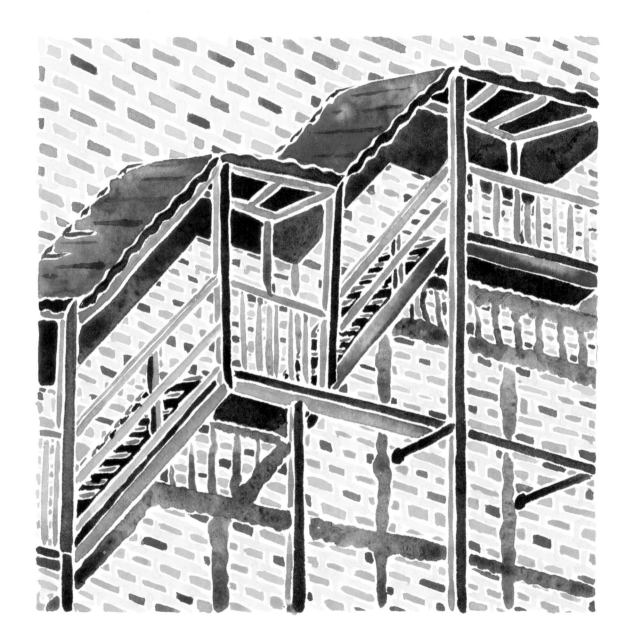

#60 ANGRY BIRDS

#61 "TOOL TOWN" HOLIDAY LIGHTS

#62 PINK PERSUASION

#63 ALL DAY BREAKFAST

#64 MAKING WAVES

#65 FRESH CUT!

#66 CHRISTMAS MISFITS

#67 WINTER STREAM

#68 CRAFT VENDOR BEAUTY QUEEN

#69 WINTER STREAM II

#70 WINTER STREAM III

#71 NOR'EASTER

#72 FROM THE SPILLWAY

#73 FROM THE SPILLWAY II

#74 NORTH AMERICAN

#75 NORTH AMERICAN II

#76 OVERARCHING THEORY

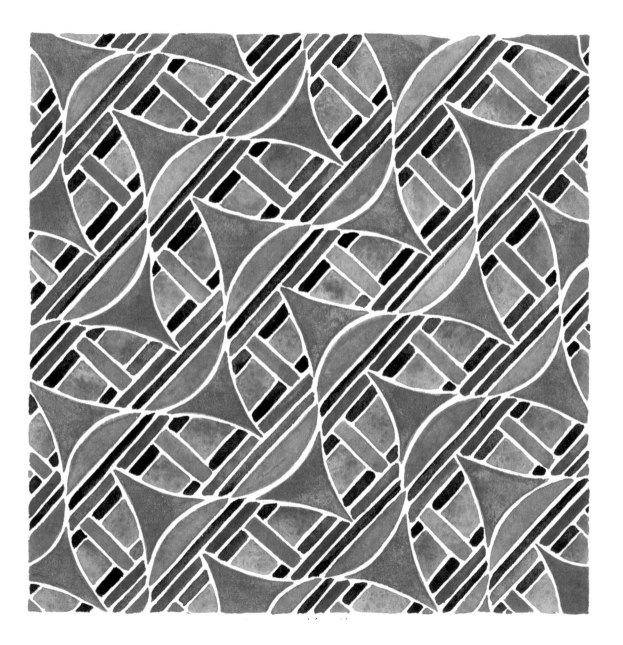

#77 GRANNY SQUARES

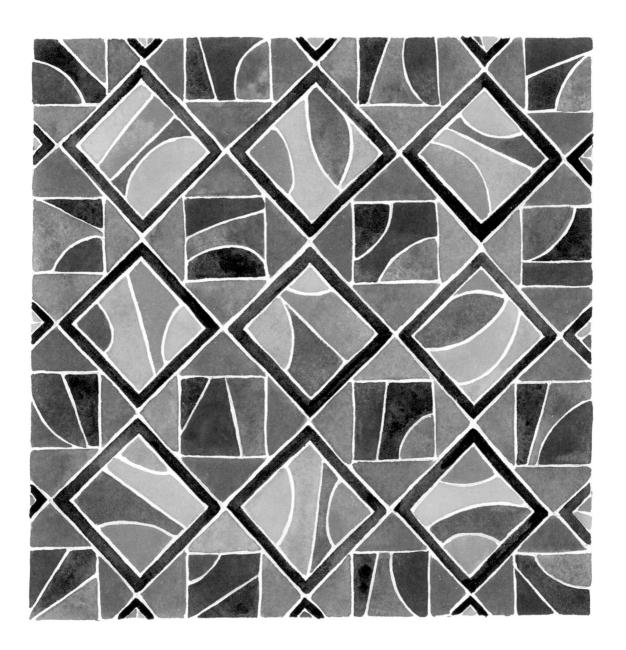

#78 Lonesome Pine Farm

#79 HEAT OF THE NIGHT

#80 LONESOME PINE II

#81 FIELD'S EDGE IN WINTER FOG

#82 COLDPLAY

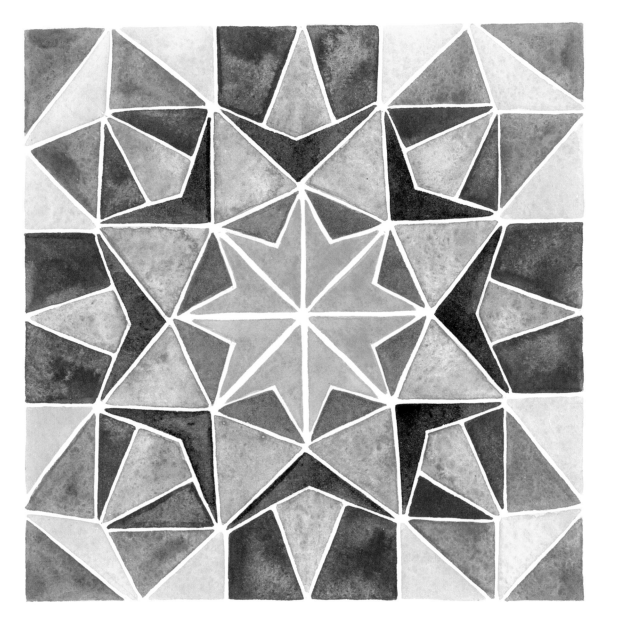

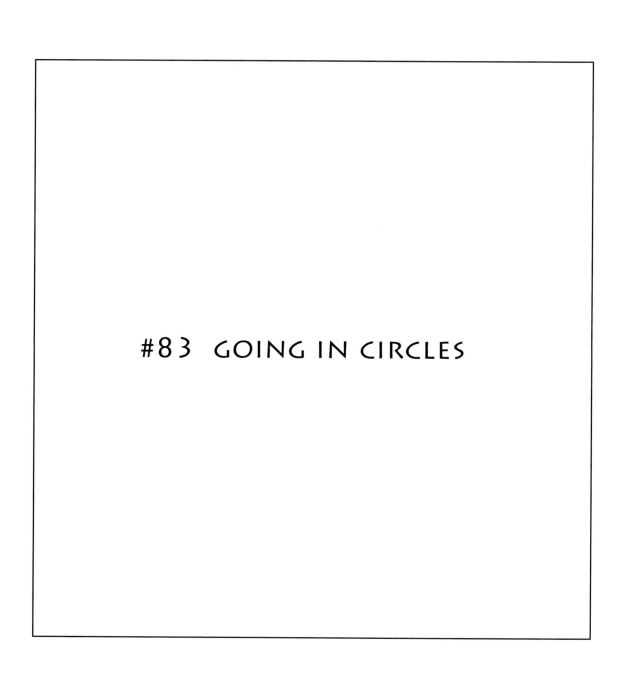

#83 GOING IN CIRCLES

#84 ASTEROID BELT

#85 THE FEELING IS MUTUAL

#86 "DON'T MESS WITH MY TUTU"

#87 ELLEN'S ORCHIDS

#88 A MATTER OF PERSPECTIVE

#89 JUST DESSERTS

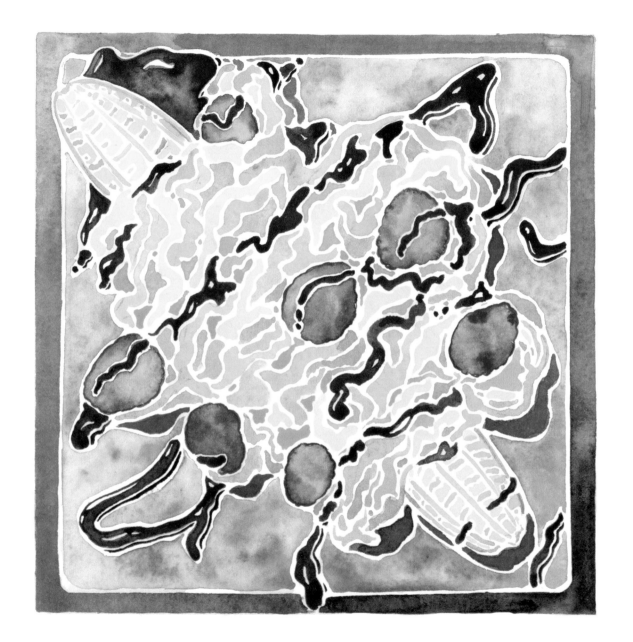

#90 FLOWERING MAGNOLIA

#91 MAGNETIC STORM

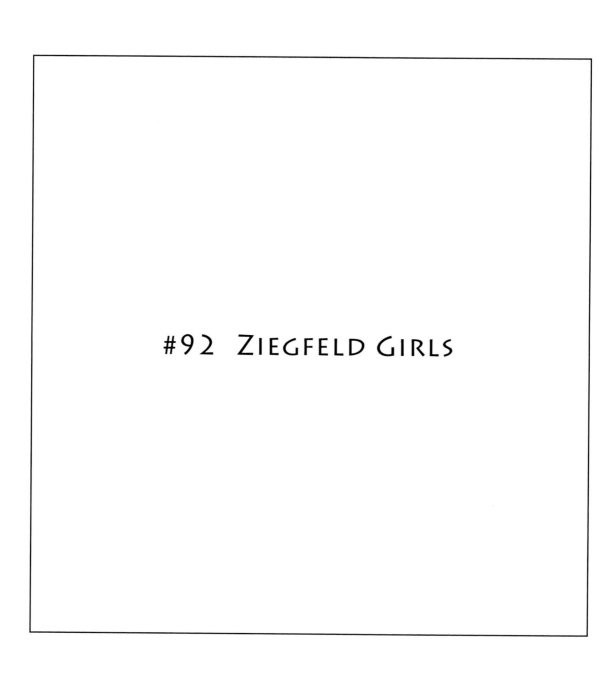

#92 ZIEGFELD GIRLS

#93 BEHIND THE MIX N' MATCH

#94 THIS RIDE TAKES 3 TICKETS

#95 POWERPLAY

#96 JOHN W. HALLOWELL GATE
HARVARD U.

#97 FLOWERING DOGWOOD

#98 SPRING PLANTING
HADLEY, MA

#99 AMERICAN INDIAN

#100 AT A CROSSROAD

#101 FORGIVE US.
WE KNOW NOT WHAT WE DO

what's more to be done?

listen, be kind, of service

this is my practice

may we walk softly

accepting of our losses

with humility

What *is* a visual haiku? "Well," says Ami, *"I made it up!* But any art that can really draw a line in the sand and express the unexpressable by expanding boundaries at an expanding rate is where the action is, is where the *universe is*. One dictionary defintion of haiku: a Japanese poem of seventeen syllables in three lines of five, seven, and five, traditionally evoking images of the natural world.

"In the spirit of visual literacy," Ami continues, "I literally conjugated the concept of haiku with a self-imposed parameter of visual expression synchronizing each watercolor to a six-inch-by-six-inch composition and from one to three hours for execution. Each image is anointed with a linguistic title that enriches your visual-literary experience.

"Voilà! The visual haiku era is upon us."

Visual Haiku • Volume One • Edition One

© 2017 by Amy Fagin

International Standard Book Number: 978-0-9916102-9-7

Library of Congress Catalogue Number:

Haley's
488 South Main Street
Athol, MA 01331
haley.antique@verizon.net • 800.215.8805